BOI

MW01290731

CLASSROOM MANAGEMENT GUIDE FOR SUBSTITUTE TEACHERS

AND NEW TEACHERS

outskirtspress

DENVER, COLORADO

TABLE OF CONTENTS

PREFACE

There are many professions that have you shadowing a person for your training. From fast food restaurants to banking, you are never handed a spatula or a teller drawer and told to have at it. So why do we do this to teachers and substitute teachers? Just having a warm adult body in the classroom isn't enough, we need to train people how to deal with a vast amount of kids in one area, oh, and all the same age. Seriously, I don't care if you are the greatest parent or grandparent on the planet; it isn't easy dealing with 20 to 30 kids the same age in one room. Think about it, you have 20 – 30, let's say, 8 year olds all in your living room without a television and only two computers. Oh, and by the way, one of them sneaks lollypops and pixie sticks in and passes them secretly around. So now you have 20 – 30 hyperactive spin tops in your living room. And no, you can't lock yourself in the bathroom until they leave.

People think that since you are an adult and they are just children or teenagers, it should be easy to control and deal with the dynamics of an entire class. They are so wrong! However, because of ignorance in society, you start to lose faith in your abilities, feel useless and possibly pathetic. Don't fret or consider running from the profession like a fleeing, screaming banshee; we have all been there, done that, and hopefully got a tee-shirt.

No matter what class you are in, they will all play you like a fiddle if you are ill-equipped with strategies to deal with the class that talks too much to the class that has disrespectful teenagers with a chip on their shoulders. Even straight A students and or elementary students can be a handful when there are more of them and only one of you. Every child has to test you at some point; I believe it's in their DNA.

For instance, I had this one subbing assignment that completely took me off guard. I mean, these were little cherubs, only second graders-8 year olds. Easy assignment, right? Well, not so much. I showed up ready to play with the little kiddies. I was at the door greeting them all as they arrived into the classroom. They took their seats and when I shut the door and walked in, the chaos started. One girl yelled, "there's a dead body in the outfield! I saw it!" Then another one chimed in, "yeah, I saw it too!"

"I saw the bloody knife!" Another student added.

"Yeah, with the fingerprints! I saw the bloody fingerprints." Another student chimed in.

Everything happened so fast, all at once, so I just stood there stymied and caught off guard from a bunch of gumbies acting out the latest crime show. Before I knew it, the students were loud, screaming and jumping under their desks. One girl, the mastermind behind the "let's play the sub" game actually yelled, "let us pray," so she folded her hands and actually began praying.

The room was completely out of control, as it was 22 excited jumping beans to one. And as their chatter grew louder, I kept thinking, I am so done. How can little children take over a class? How can an adult not control little children? What are the teachers next to me thinking? Will I be called into the Principal's office? As all of these concerns began to escalate, I began to panic, boil and fester. I wanted to shout at the top of my lungs, "shut up and get back into your seats," but as you know, the word "shut up" is a curse word in elementary school (middle school is another story). But before I raised my voice to be heard three miles away, I took a couple of deep breaths and figured that if I can't beat them, then join them.....out smart them, so to speak.

"Oh my gosh!" I gasped loudly, as I covered my mouth with my hand for a visual affect.

The students all looked my way and started to hush.

"A dead body, you say? Oh my, I've got to notify the office."

"Yes" echoed throughout the room. They were all wide eyed nodding bubble heads, as they all thought that I truly believed them and their little ploy of "play the sub to get out of work" was working.

"There's a killer out there!" Voiced one boy.

"Yes. He's still out there." Another student added.

"Oh my, you poor things." I added. "I've got to protect you, so I can't have you near a dead body. No, no, no." I gave a very sincere expression. "I'll contact the office and let them know."

"Yeah," everyone chimed in a melodramatic crescendo round.

I held up my hand to keep their attention. "And I can't have you near the body, so we'll have to cancel recess." BOOM! Stunned silence for about ten seconds.

"No." Little cries of shock and awe filled the air.

"Wait." I raised my hand with that universal attention-getter signal. "Dead body. Murderer on the loose. I can't have all of you outside with such danger."

"There's no dead body, I swear." One boy called out with others nodding in agreement.

"No, no, no, I already believe you about the dead body because I know you all wouldn't lie. I truly believe you, so we can't go out. Sorry." Palms up with a shrug.

A couple of them still tried to persuade me to take them out and convince me that they really did lie to me, but I kept at it.

"No, sorry." I had their full attention and the room was finally totally silent. "I'll tell you what, if you all do your work and are completely well behaved, I'll check with the office to see if it's clear for you to go out for recess at the end of the day."

Signed, sealed and delivered. And although it felt like an eternity, it only took a total of 10 minutes from them entering the room to the end point. After that, they worked without disruption or fooling around for the rest of the day, so I took them out the last 20 minutes of class. Additionally, I informed the other teachers that I switched recess to the end of the day, so that I may use it as a reward for being good. The other teachers were okay with it; thus, I was in control of the room at last. The other teachers noticed it also.

All in all, if I had lost control and screamed louder than the students to get their attention, I would have lost face for the rest of the day, got a terrible headache, been forced into a bad mood, and the kids would have been awful all day long. The worst part is that the other teachers would have lost faith in my classroom management capabilities. And these were only second graders, can you imagine seventh graders?

So you need to know how to deal with a class without sounding like a screaming crazy person. Although, everyone is pushed there at one point or another; coming back from the jugular popping, wild eyed, red faced, crazy stare, scary place is where you need to be in order to successfully manage a classroom. Hopefully this guide book lands you into the world of serenity, butterflies, unicorns and rainbows. Not! Well, we'll work toward a calmer day that leaves you still smiling after the kids run out of the door screaming and shoving at dismissal.

CHAPTER I
INTRODUCTION

The alarm clock goes off and you spring into action. Today is your first substitute teaching assignment and you have been preparing for this moment for a while. You have had a class about substitute teaching, and have bought many wonderful books and guides with puzzles and blank KWL charts. You have also followed the guidelines and have an ample supply of crayons, colored pencils, glue sticks, glitter and rounded scissors. Yup, you have donned your most professional outfit, are truly excited and are totally ready.

Finally, the bell rings and you stand at the doorway smiling at all of the third graders that pass through. You greet them with the cheeriest of hellos. Then the girls come out to talk to you, as they want to know all about you. *I'm a hit*, you think to yourself, as the girls surround you and want your full attention. Well, until you hear a loud thump and roaring laughter, which quickly diverts your attention to the back of the room where a boy and a chair are on the ground. The class roars with laughter, and of course some students being more dramatic than others, laugh, yell loudly and drop to the floor themselves. After you see that the boy is alright, your first thought is that the teacher next door is going to think there is a lack of control in your classroom (trust me, we all worry about this). Thankfully, you remember some of your training and raise your hand to the universal "attention getter symbol." But some of the kids ignore you and keep up with their chatter, so you clear your throat and when that doesn't work, you raise your voice to get their attention, as you have to be louder than the students for them to hear you. When they finally calm down, you blow a sigh of relief and begin class.

Now you are ready to begin class, so you start with attendance. You call each student and they all answer, so you figure all is good. Plus, you have a seating chart handy - how awesome is that?! You forward the attendance to the office and hold your trusty seating chart that has names in boxes that are in the same position as the desks. Upon gazing at the seating chart, you notice two students just chatting away. So you look at your chart and then up, confidently. "Michael and John, hush please." John keeps taking, as Michael looks up at you.

"Excuse me, John." You slightly raise your voice.

"Yes?" A boy in the front row answers.

You look on your chart and the name on that seat is Kevin. The class is giggling at this point. You feel like you are losing the class already, so you tense up a little.

"Kevin." You call and the boy talking turns around. "You are in the wrong seat; go back to your assigned seat."

"But, Mrs. Black allows me to sit here." Kevin exclaims.

"Not according to this seating chart." You say.

"She changed it."

Then a chorus of agreement echoes throughout the room, oh yes, they will all agree to that. You feel somewhat frustrated and aren't about to get into an argument with third graders. "Ok, fine for today," the kids cheer happily and you think that you have smoothed that over nicely. Unfortunately, you have set a tone for the day that will not bode well for you. For instance, the students will challenge your every authoritative action thinking that you will eventually give in, and believe me, they have a lot more energy to persuade and or dissuade you than you can imagine.

Truth be told, all kids play tricks on substitute teachers. They do it because they can, and that is the only reason they need. I'm not saying that all kids are horrible, as even the worst child is an angel when it's one on one, but when you get 20 of them together, a lot of them will feed off the Dennis the Menace student. And believe me, there are at least two in every class.

As a teacher, I would joke that we feed our kids subs (pun intended). As a sub, I definitely agreed. However, I have come across that class where all of the students were quiet and on task. I walked around looking for the battery pack on their backs. Those were the classes that renewed my faith in teaching and kept me sane. Unfortunately, the teachers didn't miss a lot of time in those classes.

For instance, I was in this one class and the students walked in, one by one, sat in their assigned seats, read the instructions on the board and got to work. I didn't know what to say or do and it happened with every class period. I thought I had died and gone to heaven. On the other hand, I had a class that I almost walked out of. The students came in extremely loud, sat wherever they wanted and actually ignored me for the most part. This was a middle school in a rough neighborhood to begin with, and of course, I was new to subbing as well as teaching altogether, so I made many rookie mistakes which they fed off of. First off, I had to shout over them to call attendance which set the tone nicely. Then when I told them that they were in the wrong seats, a few refused to move and swore that the teacher allowed them to sit there. Sadly, I lost that argument. They also bantered across the room with each other instead of doing the assignment. Luckily, they did stay in their seats since I constantly walked around the room. However, I felt like I was in a hostile environment because when I tried to control them, they took it personal and wanted to argue with me. That day, I left with such a headache and distaste for substitute teaching.

Another bad situation is when I worked in this one school and had to lock the door when the bell rang. This was for protection from troubled teenagers having access into the classroom. Which I thought was a bit drastic at first, well, before I had one student banging loudly on the door until I opened it. He was about my height with crimson red eyes and dilated pupils. I had to physically block him from entering the classroom and even had to push him out of the doorway to shut the door on him. I then had to call security. And that wasn't the worst class I subbed in for that school. The really scary one was when I had to stand at the doorway and physically block ESE students from running out of the room and down the hallways. These students wanted to fist fight in the classroom also. And better yet, one actually brought in a bag of condoms. Yes, actual condoms. I didn't take it away from her either because I asked the para-professional assigned to the room and he said to let her keep them. Sadly, I figure that was a wise decision.

These substitute assignments were very rough on me since I just graduated college and was under the illusion that all children were sweet and innocent. And they were just going to gratefully ingest all of the knowledge I would bestow upon them. Yup, I was blindsided. Well anyway, I gained a permanent teaching position within a few months after those assignments. It was in a middle school and I was greener than the most fertilized grass, which the children could smell. And of course, kids being kids, did everything in their power to watch my face turn beat red as well as shoot my blood pressure through the roof. I had to walk away after two years because it wasn't getting any better and I didn't have a grip on my classroom as well as my sanity. Walking away was the best thing for me because

I was able to reflect and analyze all of my rookie mistakes. I even swore I was done with the profession but eventually had to come back because the economy went south, and I needed income immediately. I tried subbing again and surprisingly enough, I excelled at it.

For instance, I took an assignment for a math class at a middle school that I have never been to before. The first period students saw a sub and automatically licked their chops. They started off trying to take over the class with many antics. Since this wasn't my first rodeo, and I had a couple of years to reflect, analyze and learn; I had a few tricks up my sleeve. I remained calm and cool the entire time, employed many tactics that you will learn from this book and had the class quietly doing their math work. By second period the students were still doing well; I sat in the teacher's seat and read a magazine that I brought with me (you can only get away with this in middle and high school). Then the assistant principal walked in, looked around at the students, looked at me and walked out (huh?). I thought I was in trouble and going to be on the "do not call" list (they actually have a list). I continued reading since I obviously wasn't coming back, or so I thought. The assistant principal came in again during third period, stared around the room (students were also doing math work but this time with a partner in whisper voices) and then approached me. I introduced myself as I closed my magazine. The assistant stood there with a puzzled look on her face and then asked me if I would take a two week long assignment. I was surprised and said sure. The entire ordeal was a bit puzzling to me, so I went to the next door teacher during lunch time and explained the situation, hoping to be enlightened. She told me that the last three subs didn't do well, and the last one couldn't control the class at all. The students were actually going into the teacher's refrigerator and drinking the sodas while the sub was in the room. I smiled, not because of the sub or the recognition I received, but because I was able to empathize with that sub as well as the others. I did well with the other assignment also. I even felt confident enough to take another permanent teaching position. Therefore, I am now on my sixth year (two years as team leader and this year in an alternative school) and have very strong classroom management skills. However, I still have students that try my patience every day, but regardless, I am truly grateful in every way that I've learned valuable yet so simple techniques that has made my life much easier and my career rewarding.

So budding teachers and subs, you will have those times which may have you rethinking your career. Then again, you will have those assignments and or times that will renew your faith in this profession. Regardless of circumstance, it is your reaction to their actions that will make or break your day. You can be placed in a class that feed on subs and new teachers, but do very well. And that is what this book is all about: a handbook to guide you through such difficult times and or assignments. I, like some of you, was thrown into a classroom and expected to control children that I didn't know or have some sort of relationship with. No one helped me to deal with that obnoxious student that I couldn't get on task or that student that consistently challenged my authority in front of all others. I had to handle it on my own, and if I bothered administration, they didn't want me back. It was the survival of the fittest, literally.

Although I have downplayed the student antics a little, some classes will be a challenge to all, even to the veteran parents and retired teachers. Each generation is so different from the last and there has been a radically noticeable difference in the children within the past ten years. I don't know if it's influence from television shows, more violence in movies and video games, parents working later hours or dealing with broken homes. Regardless, times have changed and you must adapt to that change or you'll be struggling to maintain order in your classroom as well as being able to teach anything. As everyone knows, you must maintain good classroom management before you can even teach.

Statistics show that half of new teachers in the profession leave within five years. The three main reasons are lack of administrative support, difficulty in creating and maintaining good classroom management and low salary. All of these feed off of each other, for example, administration doesn't want to nor has the time to discipline your classroom. If they have to leave their offices frequently to handle your classroom management problems, then they want to find someone else who can handle it. Therefore, you feel frustrated because they aren't aiding you, so you feel abandoned in a wild zoo full of angry beasts (nice picture, huh?), which can be rather scary at times. Then you feel this isn't worth the pay, hence you leave. It can be a vicious cycle if you aren't prepared for the trials and tribulations you may encounter. College has taught you the subject matter well, but the classroom management class just glossed over things and never granted you with actual guidelines or real life scenarios of how to handle the kids that spend more time and energy getting out of an assignment rather than just doing it and getting it over with. Even advanced students will find ways to get out of work. So this isn't a book about horrible children, although I have met a few that made me question, this book is about handling good kids that can try your patience to the max when they act ornery at times.

Now for the meat and potatoes of this guidebook: I have separated the chapters into helpful scenarios that will aid you in your decision making for managing your classroom. Please note that not all of them will work in every situation, as you have to be the judge of when to employ them and how to tweak them to work well with your disposition and personality. As you will note, I utilize wit and sarcasm which works well for middle school students, but not with elementary. As a sub, I do not suggest sarcasm in any class because you don't have a relationship with the students and they can get out of hand which could cross a line with the teacher-student relationship.

Another important note: today's kids are a bit tricky. Elementary kids want to please you, middle school students want to displease you and high school teens don't care either way.

CHAPTER 2 - TIP 1

FROM SECRETARY
TO CLASSROOM

When you get the attendance from the secretary or attendance clerk ask for it to be copied, so you can keep a copy in the classroom with you. They may not see the logic in you having a copy of the attendance, but tell them that being able to identify each student, all throughout the day, is a vital part of your classroom management strategy. A copy of the attendance to write on is the single most important item you will need in the classroom. You shall learn why in Tip 4: Attendance.

In addition, ask the secretary for names and numbers of the Deans, clerks in the Deans' office, team leader of the team you are substitute teaching for, nurse, front desk clerk and secretary. All of these names and numbers should be written in a chart that you can keep handy; I suggest that you carry a clipboard. Although I am sure that you will be given some sort of telephone list, you won't necessarily know the names of the specific people you need. So if you at least write it on your chart, you will be able to identify and dial quickly in a possible emergency. Do not rely on the front desk to find the people for you because a lot of times the clerk at the front desk has people he/she is dealing with as well as filtering telephone calls. Do note that if the students see that you know names and numbers without hesitation, they will perceive you as knowledgeable at what you are doing. The students do pay attention to everything you do, even though they don't seem like they're listening.

Here is a chart you may copy or recreate to suit your style.

Deparment	Name	Extension
Team Leader		
Time Out Teacher -1		
Time Out Teacher -2		
Dean 1		
Dean 2		
Dean Clerk		
Nurse		
Secretary		
Front Office Clerk		

You may get these names and numbers from the secretary except for the Time Out Teachers. Reason being, is that you don't want the secretary thinking that you are ready to toss out all of the students because she may prejudge your capabilities erroneously. Get the time out teachers' numbers once you speak to the team leader or the teachers around your classroom.

The secretary may escort you to your classroom or give you a key with a map. Regardless of how you get there, do not isolate yourself in your room. Go and ask for the team leader and speak to the teachers around you. Many times a teacher on my team has had a sub, and the sub went straight into the room and didn't pop out until the end of day. They haven't established a much needed rapport with the other teachers or team leader for help. Always remember that you are not in this alone and cannot do this alone. Even veteran teachers seek help and guidance from other teachers, so never isolate yourself.

If there isn't a team leader, or if you are subbing for the team leader, ask the teachers around you what the guidelines are for disruptive students. As some schools, especially high schools have you contact the Dean's office and or send the student there. A lot of schools utilize time out procedures with the surrounding teachers. Make sure you find that out because I didn't check in one school, and I sent a student to another class for a time out which disgruntled the secretary. So do ask, and if they do the time outs, then ask the name, room location and extension number. You may not have to send anyone out, but then again, you may have a challenging class and have to thin out the catalysts. This information is very important because you just can't kick a student out to wander the hallways. And there will be times and students that will push your limits, so if you aren't fully prepared, you may do something or say something rash. All in all, a little preparation shall make your day run a lot smoother and keep you on the "call back" list.

Another thing to ask the other teachers or team leader about is if there are any activities scheduled for that day. Will there be a fire drill and what are the procedures? Is there any kind of assembly and what are the procedures for that as well. If you are in an elementary class, check about recess. Do you go out for recess, how long and where?

You may want to create an information sheet to attach to your clipboard as well. The following chart is an example you may copy or recreate for your style.

Information to Check for	Procedure
Where to send a disruptive student(s)	•
	•
Assemblies – School Function	•
	•
Recess, if so, then what time and where?	•
	•
Do you walk students to any classes? Lunch?	•
	•
Drills : Fire, Toronado, Earthquake,	•
	•

So far, you have a clip board with an easily accessible name and extension list (again, don't rely on the general telephone directory) and a check sheet for functions, necessary movement and activities. It is important to be aware of even the most minute details because you will need to keep your focus on the students and don't need any extra surprises. If you even look lost and have to rely on the students for guidance, they will perceive you as weak and unprofessional. After that, it will be hard to save face. So be prepared to exude confidence and professionalism, and the students will look up to you, as well as respect you.

CHAPTER 3 - TIP 2

HOW TO COMMUNICATE WITH STUDENTS

Elementary children are very sensitive and want to please you. With today's television shows modeling mischievous behavior, they have been desensitized a little and aren't as innocent as they once were. They can stir up a class, dish it out so to speak, but they truly can't take it. Some students will cry dramatically when a consequence has been administered. Regardless of any sympathy you feel, don't let this deter you from reprimanding because if you don't follow through, you're toast. Remember, at this age, they have the mind set of rules and consequences which they see in black and white. And although they won't like getting into trouble for breaking the rule, they will still test you to see if you are strong enough to follow through.

Do note that elementary students do see you as an authority figure (relish the thought for it's only a short time until they move into middle school). So you must be nice, but stern. For instance, if Bobby is talking during the test to Lisa, then just say, "Yo, yo Bobbie." Just kidding. Actually, address Bobby nicely with one warning (p.s. don't tell him that it is a warning and don't number them, like this is your first warning because Bobby will try to see how many you will go up to) and say, "Bobby, focus on your test." Then, most importantly, give him up to 45 seconds to turn around. Do not jump on him if he doesn't do it immediately because some kids take a few moments to even process the order/question. However, if he does it again, tell him to move. Only give one warning and then move the child because once should be good enough to redirect, twice or more is the student trying to challenge you. Don't be mean, just look over and say, "Bobby, move over there, thank you." Remember to have a specific time out seat within the classroom. You may repeat it again if he doesn't move within the allotted time.

Lastly, don't explain every reprimand or every time out you do with the elementary student because they do know what they have done. And if you try to explain, being the nice teacher and all, the children will think you are giving them an avenue to argue or compromise the consequence. If you are a parent, then you know how well a child can manipulate any given situation. Seriously, how many homework assignments or projects have you done or seen parents do? These kids are experts. Maybe they should be negotiators before the age of 12. All in all, as a parent, you think your child is a genius because they successfully negotiated their bedtime routine, their allowance, snack items or times and had you doing their work, but as a teacher, it can be frustrating when a child wants to argue rules and get out of consequences. Do note, if you aren't stern and do give in, even once, it will be extremely difficult to gain back your authority because the little tikes won't listen until you're screaming like a banshee. And that is the last thing you ever want to do. The kids see it as comical, the administration sees it as a potential law suit and your doctor sees it as hypertension medication.

Now for a new type of animal, a fiercely beast: the middle school student. Today's generation of teenagers has changed dramatically in the past ten years; some are completely desensitized, sarcastic and even aggressive. Although, there are many very moral teenagers (they are worth their weight in gold), even they don't accept anybody as authority unless some sort of bond is present. I have heard of my most well behaved student going off on a substitute. I was completely shocked, but found out that the substitute was constantly yelling which had my student on defense. I couldn't reprimand the teenager because she sincerely thought the sub was condescending, and I couldn't side with the sub because he most likely made some mistakes because of not knowing how to speak to the hormonally challenged teenager.

First off, never scream because it's like having a starring contest with a pit bull. Parents can get away with screaming, new teachers and substitutes can't. The moment you lose control of your emotions and or tone, you are fodder. The student will report you to administration and may even make up some extra atrocities. You must be stoic in a new class, meaning, at times use please or thank you in your reprimands, always in a non-emotional tone.

Another rookie mistake is to think that you can control a teenager because you are an adult. Wrong!! You aren't their parent, and do note that a lot of today's parents can't even control their own child. I'm not being judgmental or harsh; it is a sad truth. I have had many conferences with parents and they have told me that they have done every-thing they could to no avail, and didn't know what else to do. So go in with the attitude that you are not there to control them individually, but to control the dynamics of the class as a whole. For example, if I had a chatty bunch, I didn't fight with them; I just told them to work with a partner, stay in their seats and do the assignment, as long as it wasn't a test. My suggestion to all subs is to work with them if possible. I'm not suggesting that you let the students rule the room, but don't make it hard for yourself. Teachers and administrators will view you as doing a great job if the work is done or at least worked on, room isn't trashed, students aren't screaming and disturbing other rooms and your students are in the room, seated. Teachers don't even expect all of the work to be done, well, except me. When I have a sub, I always give my students a read-ing test on a scantron and I do use the grade. Even some of my advanced students have fooled around and earned an

F, and I still put the grade in, regardless of their pleading. I let them know that it was their choice to fail, not the subs fault. After a couple of F's, the students start doing better. Whenever possible try to work with, to some degree, and not against the teenagers, so your assignment will be less stressful.

If two or three middle school students are off task, call them by name (very important which you will learn in Tip 4) and speak in a stern, not angry, tone. Let's say that John, Deiondre and Chris are off task, and John is out of his seat. "John, get back into your assigned seat ....(pause a few moments), thank you." "Deiondre, please turn around and focus on your assignment." By this time, Chris should be doing his work. If you call them gentlemen or anything else besides their name, you might as well talk to the wall because they won't listen most times. The reason it is important to call the middle school student by name is because it makes them strictly accountable for their actions, and it looks like you took the time to know their name which some do appreciate, even if they don't show it.

A lot of teachers use sarcasm in the classroom, but I do not recommend doing that for subs and new teachers. The students don't know you and may take it literally which will put them on defense. So be nice yet firm. Also if a student replies sarcastically to you, say "do not speak to me that way." Don't let it go because the student will continue to speak to you in that manner which may escalate to disrespect. Be stern, not angry and if they continue to disrespect or argue with you, do not argue back with any student. If they try it, get them out and quickly. Don't yell, especially out of frustration, just calmly say, "Please go to …… (time-out teacher's name)." Remember, they will move slowly to save face with their peers, but they will leave. And don't say anything else, trust me, anything you say, even sarcasm will be repeated and probably twisted. Just go on with the assignment like nothing happened.

Remember, you are there to teach or cover a class, not be abused. If you speak kindly, not condescendingly or arrogantly, most students will respond. It's like the kids can smell arrogance a mile away and if they sense it, they will be a challenge for you. I did make that rookie mistake in the beginning of my career and had many problems because of it. I came in with the attitude of, I'm an adult, I have a degree and you are an ignorant teenager. Yup, they handed me my arse. So don't make that mistake.

Even the worst acting children are still children and you must remember that. They will challenge you just because, so don't give them a reason.

Now, we graduate to high school which is so much easier. Those students are usually focused because they want to graduate. In addition, the students are at the age of being able to drop out, so administration doesn't put up with a lot of problems. The only thing I can say about high school is to speak politely to them, call them by name and give them a little bit of leeway. Meaning, I don't chase down cell phones, I just tell them to put them away. I don't mind if they have a snack. I've actually seen 11th and 12th graders eat a full breakfast. As long as they bring it in themselves, I really didn't care because at that age, they are generally responsible. I just asked them to make sure that they throw the trash away and clean up their mess which they always did.

I remember one assignment in a 12th grade class which two boys were talking during a test, so I called them by name and asked them to focus on their test. They were amazed that I knew their names since I have never subbed with them before. One student said, "Wow, my teacher still doesn't even know my name." It was October. I just said, I can read minds and went back to doing the work I brought with me.

So all in all, don't go into the classroom joking and laughing, be very stern and even stoic in some cases. Don't start off with a big smile, but end the class with one. The reason being is that this generation is more fixated on being "cool," and they will see a very enthusiastic disposition as a weakness. Speak nicely, repeat if necessary, give wait time, and don't allow the situation to get out of control so that you lose your head. Then you will be smiling large at the end of the day.

CHAPTER 4 - TIP 3

ENTERING THE CLASSROOM

Something as simple as entering the room can set the tone for your classroom management. Since you are expected to stand at the door and smile as the students enter your room, you don't really know what the students are doing inside the room. You can't see in the middle of them if they are gathered around each other, and they won't hear you calling from the door, especially if they are running around the room. And yes, even 8th grade students still run around the room. Unless you have an exceptional class, (they really do exist) you need to assert some sort of control without leaving your post.

I was in an elementary classroom one day and stood at the door to greet each student as they entered. In the back of the room, two third graders were running and jumping on a bean bag until it popped. A few students were standing around chatting and some were in seats. I couldn't see completely inside the room because students were everywhere in the classroom and hallway. There were too many distractions. Students were talking to me at the doorway, asking me questions in the hallway and teachers were talking as well. Veteran teachers already have their students trained to enter the room and sit, but a sub or new teacher doesn't have that kind of control, especially on a one day assignment. So I was left to explain why the teacher's bean bag was busted. Thus I never received a call from that teacher again.

The same can happen with a middle school class as well. If students enter the room on their own while you are standing at the door with many distractions, the students have already taken over the class. Middle school boys still chase girls around the room and the girls still antagonize the boys which can sometimes turn into a fight between them. In addition, you sometimes have couples in the same class, and if unsupervised, they will start kissing which is against school policy. Therefore, it behooves you to have some sort of procedure in place to avoid furniture getting destroyed, students getting hurt, or school policy being broken.

The only problem with high school students is the couple thing. You need to watch them a bit, but you are pretty safe at the door most of the time. Some high schools don't even require you to be at the doorway which is a lot easier on you.

Well, I have spoken about potential problems that may arise, so let's begin with a possible solution that will work well in elementary as well as middle school. It is so simple yet effective. And I've learned and modeled this from a veteran teacher that had superb classroom management. I do employ this tactic even as a permanent teacher, as I always do this at the beginning of the year as part of my procedures. I still do this in some of my classes that I cannot trust to enter the room without problems.

I have the students line up at the door while I stand in the doorway. I don't have them enter until I let them in, two or three at a time. Just stand at the door and say, "please form a line" to the first few students that approach. Then say, "please get in line" to the students that join in. And when the hallway settles down, let them in by twos or threes, depending on the dynamics of the group. If the students are standing there nicely, you can even go up to four at a time, but if they are already acting up in line, pull those students aside and then continue with only two at a time. You are being polite, yet controlling the situation before it even starts. And if any students are going to act up, they will have already started in line, so you can watch them in class and already have a game plan.

Lining up the students is great because you are at your duty post, the students already see that you are organized, plus the other teachers take note that you have things under control from the beginning and will seek to call you again. Additionally, the students entering are more inclined to sit in their assigned seats. It should only take up about two to three minutes. In addition, don't wait until each one is seated before sending the next group; just make sure they are at their desks. It does take them a few seconds to get organized, so the other group can already get started. And do note, this doesn't guarantee that the students are sitting in their proper designated seat (you will learn about that in Tip 4), but it may set a calmer and more collective tone to start off with.

CHAPTER 5 - TIP 4

ATTENDANCE:
WITH OR WITHOUT A
SEATING CHART

(Please note that although the use of he/him as gender neutral pro-nouns is often discourage, I am using it because it is too confusing to keep using he/she or him/her)

You have a student that is beyond defiant; you ask him to please be quiet but he won't. He gets out of the seat and disturbs others. Since you don't know his name, you say, "young man," but the student doesn't listen. Since you can't call the student by name, the student acts like he is invisible to you and can do whatever he wants to without recourse. That is what a lot of students think and sometimes it works out well for them because the sub is too flustered to correct the situation or waits for the period to be over which is too late. So the student leaves sans consequence which reinforces that behavior for the next time.

Moreover, identifying the student by name will alleviate some issues. And that is where a copy of the attendance is imperative. Some teachers will leave you a copy of the roster with pictures of the student, but don't count on that. You need to be able to identify the student in case you have to send him to another class, write him up or address him in any way. The student will not only see it as a sign that you are capable, but he will also think that you cared enough to take the time to know his name. It will also deter some of the bad behaviors because now the student is identifiable and accountable for his actions.

I have been caught a couple of times with the no name game, meaning, students have given me a wrong name on purpose and then chuckled when I corrected them with the false name. It was all a game to them and very frustrating for me. I have even tried to remember the students name or asked a couple of quiet students for help. That didn't work because the quiet student was too afraid of retaliation from the misbehaved student to get involved. And trying to remember names when you are only there for a day is way too much effort. The day saving method I am about to bestow upon you is one that I employ at the beginning of every year, and I wind up knowing all 100 of my students' names by the end of the second week.

Now this is where you utilize the copy of the attendance. Take attendance on your copy first; you can transfer over the absentee marks to the original afterwards. At this point, do not even try to quiet down the students if they are talking. It is important that they aren't paying too much attention to what you are doing because even the students that may give you problems will answer when you call their name. This method will take about five minutes, but they are minutes you will gain from on task behavior.

When you call a name and they answer, look for some kind of distinguishing feature that will help you identify the student quickly. For instance, if you call Christian and he is wearing black glasses and has spiky blonde hair, write at least one of those items to identify him quickly. If John has Clooney style hair and Ashley has dredlocks, write it. At one point, you will have to address even your quietest student, so know their names as well. For instance, Maria is a very quiet and sweet girl and you want her to pick up the papers. She will respond very favorably when you are able to say, "Maria, would you please pick up all of the papers," and "class, Maria shall gather the papers; please make sure you have your names on them."

This is especially helpful if the students are in the wrong seat and there is a seating chart. Do take in mind, if the students are working quietly with very low voices and are on task, I generally don't bother them if they are good and respectful. And if a couple of students start getting loud and off task, I will address them by their names. I will say something like, "Chris and Sean, I know you are in the wrong seats, but I won't mind if you stay on task and do your work quietly or with whisper voices. Are we good?" Not only will they be in shock that you called their names, but you also knew they were in the wrong seats. This is the age where they believe that they are so much smarter than all adults. You outsmart them without being arrogant or condescending and the students will show you respect and listen.

It is essential that you tear up or shred the list by the end of the day. You don't want anyone to read your descriptions of the students because someone will always be offended. I wrote descriptions for my sub on the names that I didn't have pictures for and I wrote "popular black boy" and that student said something to me about it. He said why did you write that, so I asked him, "would you have preferred nerdy, ugly white boy?" He just laughed and walked away. I have that relationship with my students, but as a sub you don't. I am truly convinced that the students have tick marks on their belts when they run off a sub. I have actually been told one year by a group of 7th graders that they have successfully run off 9 subs the previous year. I was appalled that they talked about it like it was a badge of honor. It is sad, but students use that as a power trip.

So anyway, shred the copy by the end of the day, not before because at some point of the day you may run into that student again and need to know his name.

CHAPTER 6 - TIP 5

HANDLING THE PROBLEM STUDENT

A lot of subbing assignments will land you with at least one difficult child that will have a lot of energy to push every one of your buttons. However, there have been some assignments where I was in a school that all of the children were wonderful. I call them the "Stepford" Students, after the movie "Stepford Wives" in 1975. Those are the classes where the subs camp out at the front desk. But for the most part, a lot of assignments will have you in normal to problematic classrooms, as those teachers tend to be out more which we consider to be much needed "mental health" days.

One assignment had me in a class that one boy, I still remember what he looked like, challenged me in every way possible. He found reasons to walk around the classroom and disturb others. He spoke to everyone around him, even if I moved his seat he found someone new to talk to. I spent too much time and energy fighting with him, so the class acted out as well. The students thought that since he got away with it, they needed to try it also. Even middle school students have a sense of fairness at times. So because of this one student, my class was out of control and I had so much undo stress trying to reel them back in. In addition, I lost respect arguing with that student.

You will find these students in all grades, and I have found that the ones in middle school were the easiest to deal with. I know that sounds contradictory, but how I tell you to deal with them will demonstrate that middle school students are the easiest in some cases.

When you take an assignment in an elementary school, you have the students all day long and cannot kick out students for the entire day, so you will have to deal with the disruption regardless. And one problem could be that the student did not have his ADHD/ADD medication, so the child cannot help his/her behavior. Unfortunately, the parent not giving him the medication for any reason has now become your cross to bear.

First of all, address the disruptive elementary student by name. Calling the student by his name personalizes it, so he will be more apt to listen. Then either move his color, card, pin, or give him up to ten minutes time out during recess. The teacher will have a structured consequence for bad choices and you must follow it and most importantly, do not give in. The students will always, and I mean always try to dissuade you from following through. All students will become miniature lawyers and try to argue with you;

they will try to comprise with, "if I'm good for the rest of the day will you...", and they will even shed the faux tears. Yes, they will try at least one of those things, if not all, and if you give in then you may as well hand them the keys to the room. If you give in, your word won't mean anything afterwards. The students will be tremendously happy and you'll feel the love, well, until they break another rule and no matter what you say or do, they will argue and challenge you. And they will beg and plead with you endlessly until you give in, which you will, because your will was bent the first time and they have much more energy and persistence than you do. You must adhere to the rules and administer the proper consequences although you feel bad looking at their sad faces. You never need to yell or get frustrated, just state the rule and the consequence very calmly and politely. If they try to argue, just say "you knew the rule, but made a bad choice," and keep to that. Some kids will do the crocodile tears, some will even throw a temper tantrum, but they will all get over it within a minute or two if you don't react. Your day shall go much smoother if you be the adult/teacher, not the ever so doting mother/father/grandmother/grandfather figure.

Now onto the middle school lovelies: be swift to end it before it begins. First off, don't try to control them; you are a stranger with no personal connection with them, so anything you say or do may be dealt with defensively. They already have their guard up with any adult that's not their parent, relative, teacher or personal friend. I am sorry, but the days of "respecting adults just because" are over. This generation of teenagers is a new breed and is more sarcastic, defiant and defensive than the older generations. Now, don't get me wrong, there are a lot of great kids out there and some just take getting to know. I have dealt with and punished kids that I wouldn't recommend anyone turning their back on; however, I had been successful in my dealings because I had a good teacher relationship with the students. As their teacher, I've had to prove myself time over time. I've had to demonstrate strength, zero tolerance for bad choices, patience, politeness and respect. I always talk to them politely, call them by name and most of all, have never given in.

When dealing with the middle school child never be arrogant, as I swear they could smell arrogance from a mile away and you automatically become their personal challenge. Remember all kids have value, regardless of how bad they act, but don't try to counsel with them because you'll get personal conversations without work getting done. In addition, don't try to control them because they will fight back. I find that a lot of this generation's parents don't even have control over their own children, so why should you: a stranger. The only thing that you are there to do is to control the environment, not the individual child.

If a student enters your room and starts up, meaning, walking or running around the room, talking during a quiet assignment, trying to stir up the other students and/or class, kick him out after the second warning. Simple as that! Don't argue with him because if you try to justify your point then you have already lost. Just say, "Johnny, -state the infraction stoically (no emotion added)- kindly pick up your books and go to –name of time out teacher-. Thank you." Also the student will most likely try to argue his innocence, even if he knows he was in the wrong-don't let him. Cut him off. I say "good point, but goodbye." Oh, and he may say bad things to rile you up, just don't take it personal or get upset. Continue dismissing him calmly. Don't smile, don't pop a jugular and **do** give the student up to a minute to start moving before you repeat the order to leave.

The reason you give the students a minute is because they are at the age that they need to save face with their friends. I know that they shouldn't be openly defiant, and it is disrespectful, but don't fight it, as you will need to pick and choose your battles in order to have a good day. When the minute arises and they still haven't moved, open the door and stand at it while saying, "Johnny, go to –name of time out teacher-. Thank you." Do note that if the student refuses to leave, then get the team leader or the closest teacher near you. Let them deal with their student, as they know that student. Simply prop open the door and walk to the next teacher or team leader. They will come out in a flash, most of the time, or they will direct you to the person you need. If you are unable to leave your classroom (they will straighten up the moment you get someone else, usually) then send a student to get the team leader or teacher. You must and I say must send them out or get them removed even if they have you questioning your decision. You don't need to be mad, mean or even write them up, just remove them and it will send a message to the rest of the class that you aren't there to play games with them. If you lose your temper and yell, they will find it amusing, so remove the person before anyone else has a chance to join in. Even if you feel bad or wonder if you did the right thing, still do it because the student will show you respect the next time that you are assigned there.

In time you may run into that one student that tries to get out of punishment by calling you a racist. Yes, someone sometime will use it, so don't get offended. Just remain calm and stoic while removing that student. It usually is best to not even respond, although, I have responded with, "no, I'm an ageist; I don't like anyone under 25." They usually don't know how to respond to that one.

Now onto the high school student: treat them the same as the middle school student, although you may need to send them to the dean and not to another teacher for time out. You'll have to ask the policy, as each high school is different. I never really had a problem with high school students because the really bad ones have usually dropped out before they advanced to higher grades. Again, don't argue, give them up to two warnings and just remove them swiftly while being very calm and pleasant. Most of all, address them by name as well.

Although I have you tossing out students like potato sacks, don't toss out more than one (sometimes two) per class. If you act within the first three minutes of any mishap, you will stop the situation from spinning out of control. And other students won't have a chance to join in; therefore, you will gain control of the environment.

However, there will be times when it seems that you have no control over the class. The students are bantering back and forth, doing what they want, even though you have made several unsuccessful attempts to stop them. Plus most of the class has joined in with the blatant defiance. Unfortunately, you can't toss out the entire class. You are made to feel helpless and inadequate. Don't! Before you lose your patience and start screaming out of frustration and possibly anger because they have all joined forces against you, pause for a moment. Just stand or sit quietly and watch them as though you were watching a movie (that actually unnerves them). You have a chance to collect yourself and they will be thrown totally off guard and even perplexed by what you are doing or not doing. Just watch them and within five minutes the numbers will start to dwindle. Only the ones with the true agenda to disturb the class and you will be left. Then say to the remaining two or three, "outside now." Stern yet calm. The troublemakers won't know what to think as you escort them out of the door. Remember to position yourself at the door so that you are able to see the class. Let the students know that they can stop it and walk into the class quietly or be removed. Look at them each for a moment before saying "am I clear?" Most will comply, but you may have that stubborn student, to which, you say "goodbye" and point to the time out door. Watch him leave and then let the others back into class. Do document who had to be removed and why so the regular teacher has a chance to deal with them if he chooses.

Generally, if you have control over the classroom, the teachers and administrators will note that you have good classroom management and will make sure to have you in their class/school again. Remember, it's the teachers and secretary that hire you, not the students, so they are the ones that need to like you. If my students love a sub, I automatically worry what the sub is doing that I should be concerned about. For instance, are the students ruling the classroom or is the sub sugaring them up for acceptance. If either one is happening, then I don't want that sub, plus the other teachers that have to deal with the sugar high all day will kill me if I have that sub back.

CHAPTER 7 - TIP 6

CONSTANT BANTERING/ HORSEPLAY/FIGHTING

Middle school students are notorious for teasing each other which sometimes gets out of hand because someone always gets offended and then it turns into a fight. They are the most brutal of the three schools; therefore, you must stop it immediately. Even though they will swear to the holy heaven that they are just playing and they do it all of the time, don't allow it to continue. I have seen best friends get into fist fights one minute and then become best friends again after they have already caused a lot of stress for the teachers and their parents. They just don't get it, yet they continue with their totally dysfunctional behavior because they are hormonal teenagers. There is no rhyme nor reason for half of the things they do, so don't waste your time explaining the rules or procedures. They already know and don't care; just let them know that it isn't going to happen in the classroom while you are present. I know this sounds tough, but you have to appear tough because they will disrupt the classroom, not do their work and possibly fight. You must protect yourself as well as the student body from harassment and stop it.

Now that I told you that you need to stop it before someone gets angry or hurt, I probably should tell you how. For instance, no one should come into class horse playing, especially if you have them enter the class a few at a time. However, there may be some that still want to play around, either by chasing each other around or verbally slamming on each other. So you will have to be polite, but stern. Remember that you already set the tone by having them enter a couple at a time, so most will get that, but as you know, kids will be kids. For example, Chris and Sam enter your room, and of course, they are not in their assigned seats. You could have probably overlooked that, but they won't stop verbally slamming on each other and others, which they find loads of fun. Unfortunately the entire class attention is on them, so you are losing control.

When you get into class, take attendance before you address the bantering in order to know their names. If you ignore the bantering while you take attendance, they will most likely answer. When you finish the attendance, call them by name (all of them) and pull them aside, either to your desk or outside the door and say, "You need to stop teasing each other and other classmates. Everyone needs to focus on the assignment, so save the play for later. Are we clear?" They'll most likely agree. Also, the students will usually respond well since you took the time to talk to them on the side as opposed to calling them out in class. However, if they continue while in their seats, after your talk, then say, "if you aren't able to stop, then I need you to go to Mr./Mrs. _____ room." Remember to keep your tone low, your demeanor calm and your attitude indifferent. If they reach a third time, remove the one (or two) that is the most adamant about teasing. And of course that student will argue that the other students aren't getting removed and that you are picking on him/her. Do not argue, just say, "I'm not going to argue with you, and I need to split you up, so no one has to be written up, that's all. Thank you for being the better person. Goodbye" and hold the door open. Leave it at that, don't argue or say anything else. However, if the student still tries to argue, then say, "If you continue, then I'll have to write you up. Thank you and goodbye." Still hold the door open for him to leave, and give him a good amount of space to pass through. He should leave by this time, if not, then prop the door open and ask the other teacher to remove the student. If that happens, then you must write them up for being "Openly Defiant."

Do the same for high school, yet handle elementary students differently. If they start bantering/verbally slamming each other (and some will do it), then you need to call the main one or two instigators up to the desk and say, "stop teasing your classmates." And when they continue, because you know they will, call one student by name (the instigator) and say, "I told you to stop. If this continues then I'll have to (move your clip/card to the lower level of behavior, write your name on the board, or whatever behavior support the teacher uses)." Now some students will end it right there, but there are some that will challenge to see if you will follow through. If they push it, you must, and I repeat you must administer the consequence. Regardless of tears and begging, you can't give in because if you do, then every child will be acting out and challenging you. Believe it or not, even the little ones will lose respect for you when you don't do what you say you are going to do. These kids have had people going back on their word enough, so they need you to follow through, even if they cry, plead or argue. And once they know you mean business, you can treat them all very nicely and maybe even slip in something artsy or add a couple more minutes to recess time.

In regards to fighting, let the other middle school and high school teachers get into the middle of those. Believe me, I have broken up a lot of fights, but I know the kids and have insurance if I get hurt. You don't, so have a student get help and tell them to separate. The only thing that you are required to do is to say, "stop fighting." Any more than that may get you hurt. Many teachers get hurt, and if you get hurt the students will talk about it for the rest of the year. You'll be known as the sub that got his/her butt beat by a student. Oh, the story will be embellished a lot too. I kicked a student out of my class for good; had her transferred and she told everyone that she hit me. It wasn't worth fighting the rumors, so I just let them die out. In addition, if you let them know that the deans are on their way, the rest of the students will separate them quickly. That has worked a couple of times when I subbed. But then again, you have those UFC matches where the deans and possibly school resource officer (SRO) have to deal with. Don't fret because no one is going to look at you like you did something wrong, as these students are already well known, and the teachers most likely got wind that something was already brewing. They were just waiting for the apocalypse or for it to fade away.

Now the fighting of elementary students is a bit different. You most likely will have to separate them which will be a lot easier if they are young. I suggest you follow the middle school tip above if they are fourth and fifth graders. The smaller ones will be easier to separate and keep a part. Have them separated to each side of the room until administration comes to collect them. Hit the call button or have a student get someone from the office to pull them out because administration will want to have them checked and call parents. Administration can't afford for the little ones to be hurt or tattered and not give the parents a heads up at least.

You usually don't have many fights in high school or elementary because high school students can go off campus and elementary students aren't as aggressive yet. Middle schools are where the most fights take place because they are hormonal and have adult relationships which they aren't mature enough to handle. Now, I'm not suggesting that you carry a chair and a whip when you go to middle school, although I always tell people that my profession is Zoo Keeper. Anywho, middle school usually isn't bad, but they are the most challenging of the three schools. However, if you know how to handle kids and follow the tips I have explained, then middle school won't be a problem. You may even like it. I actually prefer middle school and high school over elementary. The teenagers always got my jokes and witty sarcasm, but the elementary kids just looked at me like I stole their cookie.

Do note, that I have given you many scenarios for the bad stuff that could happen, but you may not have classes that verbally banter or fight. You may say stop and they do it immediately, or they may not even do any of that at all. These tips are to help you if you encounter those problems and need solutions. Think of this book as a fire drill which prepares you on how to act if you ever do come across a problematic classroom and or student(s). So don't get scared off, just be armed with lots of knowledgeable tips to promote excellent classroom management.

CHAPTER 8 - TIP 7
INHERENT AUTHORITY

A lot of subs enter the classroom, read the teacher's instructions and try to enforce the procedures to the teacher's standards. This is wonderful and all, but do remember, you don't need to create a stressful day for yourself. The teacher may have the students working quietly all of the time which will be easy for him/her because they have spent many months establishing those routines; however, the kids will break those rules since the teacher is away. And you will spend more time fighting with the students to keep a quiet class. Although, some classes will do their work quietly, others won't, so work with what you have. If there is an assignment, other than a test, I usually allow the students to work with a shoulder partner and talk in low voices. Now make sure you say their shoulder partner on either side of them, not their friends because they will all join their friends and do nothing, except socialize. Of course they will plead and beg that they work well with their friends and fight with their shoulder partners. Don't give in! I repeat: Don't give in! You will regret it in most cases. They will not do their work and it will be too involved and stressful to move them all back. Just tell them no and if they can't get along with their shoulder partner then work alone. Remember, the teacher will be more impressed if the work is actually done. In addition, if they finish their work early on a test, I usually give them a word search that I brought in.

Additionally, I have read the textbook with the whole class at times. There are some classes that can't read and or comprehend well enough to read the chapter and answer questions. You will know because you'll find that this class is extremely off task and nothing seems to help. They will all need your immediate attention at the same time and be very demanding to the point of confusion and frustration for you. So, to save yourself a headache and to help the students, read it with them. You read a paragraph or two then call on students to read a paragraph each. Pause at times to discuss what you or they have read and continue reading. You may have to go over and explain the questions with them as well. Remember, a lot of classes will work independently, but there are some classes that you will need to work with in order to maintain focus.

Furthermore, if you utilize Tip 3 along with Tip 4, then the students will know that you are organized and in charge, so they will do the work, most of the time. In addition, a majority of the teachers won't mind if you allow the students to work with a shoulder partner because some students may need that extra help. And since you helped or provided help, the students will work with you as well. However, don't be too lax with the rules because they will take advantage of you and then you will have to answer to administration why you have groups of students running around campus.

Speaking of running around, the students will all have to go to the bathroom since their teacher is away. Make sure it is only one at a time, not one boy and one girl, but one student at a time. Let the student know that they need to be quick because other students can't go until they return. This will prompt most of them to not fool around too much. A lot of times they just want to stretch their legs and text in the bathroom. Don't worry about being the phone police; it's not worth the fight because they will only get their phone back soon enough. As a sub and a teacher, I just tell them to put it away if I see the phone out. I stopped confiscating phones a long time ago; however, I do take the phone if they don't put it away or I catch them on it. Most of the time, they'll put it away. In a rare case that a student refuses to put the phone away and/or won't give it up, call the dean's office. They'll take the phone and the student will get into more trouble.

There were times when I allowed the students to listen to ipods or such when they finished their assignment. As long as it isn't the entire class period or half the period; about ten minutes is good. You will have to judge whether it's okay with the class or school policy. I mean, if the school has a strict policy of no electronics then don't bother, but if it isn't a big problem, no one will crucify a sub for a little leeway, especially if the students are doing their work, staying in their seats and being respectfully quiet.

With the elementary students, I have created books with their math lessons at times. What I would do was to take printer paper and fold a couple of pieces into a booklet and have the students create simple word problems with their math. This works great for elementary because they can draw out the cookies, candy, or fruit to add/subtract, plus they can decorate the booklet. This makes the math lesson much more interesting and the teachers love it. Do that if you have the time and know how. In addition, you may get creative with a science, social studies, reading or writing lessons as well. The elementary students love it and it impresses the teacher.

CHAPTER 9

REFLECTION

Hopefully this guide has helped you through a lot of problems you may encounter throughout your substitute teaching and permanent teaching career. As a lot of substitutes make this their career since they can afford to live on the pay and have other medical benefits. In return, their schedule is always flexible and they don't have the added burden of writing lesson plans, creating classwork and grading tests. Hence substitute teaching can be a rewarding job, as sometimes you are able to teach the students something as well as reach the students that can benefit from your individual knowledge. Moreover, teachers may benefit from these tips as well. Start off the year with them, employ them whenever needed and you shall have control of your class and be able to teach.

There are going to be days and assignments that will have you rethinking your career or fondness of children; however, this guide shall help you through those days. In addition, if you utilize these tips, you will be able to handle very difficult assignments with ease. You will be able to handle classes that have terrorized other subs, and you will gain the respect of teachers and administrators alike. Furthermore, the students will get to know you and respect you because they will become familiar with you and your boundaries, especially since the school staff will be seeking you out.

When you follow these tips, you will most likely have an orderly classroom and have the opportunity to get to know the children of today. As the children of today are so different from your generation; you'd be surprised what differences a decade can make. You'll gain insights of how they view the world and the people around them and even learn that they aren't so tough once you get to know them. This generation is very fierce, to which I actually see adults completely walk the other way if they encounter a group of teenagers. I just walk right through them and smile. Once you learn how to handle them, speak to them, and show them respect as you command (not demand) respect, the generation gap may not be so bad.

Even though I have spent the last eight chapters in-structing and demonstrating how to deal with the students, now I shall tell you some insights about teachers. First off, always remember that the teachers and administrators are the ones that are going to hire you, so make sure to please them. For example, I have seen many subs come in and bribe the kids with candy in order to maintain classroom management. This is a total fallacy because if you give kids candy, then they will be on a sugar high and you won't be able to control the room at all. Also, the kids will see you as a vending machine and not have respect for you whatsoever. And the teachers won't want you even around their area because they will have to deal with the sugared up kids after they leave your class. So don't, and I repeat DON'T bring in candy as a classroom management aide. I don't even recommend bringing in candy at all because it will cost you a lot of money as well as respect.

Therefore, for success overall, follow the classroom management tips, be kind, yet stern, don't bride the kids and command respect. If you have good classroom management, stress free days and other opportunities will open up. So good luck and happy subbing.

CPSIA information can be obtained at www.ICGtesting.com
Printed in the USA
BVOW08s0332130815

412992BV00003B/255/P